BAD GIRL

The Guide To Female Power

ALLORA SINCLAIR

Cuckoo
Publishing

BAD GIRL - The Guide To Female Power

©2021 by Allora Sinclair

Front Cover Illustration by: OlgaSusIO

WHAT THE HELL?

B ad girls finish first. There. I said it. You don't need to read anything else.

But wait, there's more? Yes, a lot more. Our world's values have changed so much. Think about the inability of women to vote in an election less than 100 years ago. The designated water fountains for visible minorities in the 50s and 60s. The 'rebellious' mom that went to work, while daddy stayed at home with the kids in the 90s. Today, we are still moving for a harmonized and fair society, placing gender, race, sexual orientation, and religion as irrelevant to the individual. We are who we are. No preconceived stereotype is cool or acceptable.

Yet, the riots continue. Most CEOs continue to be men. The inclusion of acknowledged gay marriages still withheld in many parts of the world and states. Cannabis is legal in one place, but not another. It's all changing, but in various ways and at various speeds.

The bottom line is, society does everything possible to resist change, even when they are last to the party. Change is scary. It's different. It's not the way it used to be. To that, I say DEAL WITH IT. It does not matter if you like it or even agree with it. It's only a matter of time.

They have built everything in our culture over thousands of years. Today, we have a speed limit on our highways. Why? To avoid collisions at high speeds. This safety measure is in place based on our current limitations. But what happens when driverless cars become the norm? (You know it's coming) What happens when every single car is controlled to interact with every other single car to get from A to B safely? Our speed limits will conceivably become infinite. We just don't have the technology for it yet. For women, their traditional role was to stay home, be subservient to their husbands, do the cooking, and cleaning and be the primary caregiver of offspring. They needed it to survive.

The historical role of women changed largely out of necessity (World Wars and increased cost of living requiring a second income). But the change in roles has not brought a change in values. Women are still secondary to men.

Don't believe me? Walk into any hospital and see how many doctors are female. Try a courtroom. See many female lawyers? How about boardrooms? Let's peek in on the demographics of the shareholders. The boys' club is sadly still alive and well.

I guess women are just not smart enough? No, that can't be it. Maybe they just don't work as hard or as well? Nope. Still no validity there. Ah, I got it. It's because they're too pretty and dumb to do a man's job? WTF ladies. Wake up and look. This is no longer acceptable for anyone under any circumstance. Yet we seem to embrace the notion that being female has some designation of being genetically suited for a supportive role only?

How does all this fit into being a bad girl you ask? Simple. From birth, we program girls to be good little compliant girls that support their knight in shining armor. Take a second and think back to the first ten years of your life. Think of what cartoons you watched, movies you saw, books you read, lessons they taught you. They encouraged boys to push the envelope while girls were mostly there to help or look pretty.

This has slowly changed in the last 15 years, but anyone over the age of 25 can relate to what I'm saying. Sadly, it's no one's fault. It's just the way it was. But it does not have to be that way anymore. No one wants it to be that way anymore. The problem is, it locks us in a mindset of how things are supposed to work. Most people (men and women) are blissfully unaware of the deep programming that has been embedded into our values and beliefs.

This is where being a bad girl enters the picture.

Just the name 'bad girl' has all kinds of negative connotations attached to it. Ewe, I don't want to be a bad girl. That's.... bad. Right? So, I guess we associate the same negative attachment to the 'bad boy'? What? No, no, no. The bad boy is hot. He's a hunka hunka burnin love? Well, that makes perfect sense, right?

Not even a tiny bit does bad boy/bad girl seem to cast the same kinds of emotions or associations. And yet, here we are reading a book about bad girls, and why it's a good thing.

The bad girl's movement is coming. It's been coming

for a long time. Only now, people are talking about it boldly and openly. No longer are the days of the private conversations between two girlfriends discussing their current reality and the life they wanted. The freedom of being a man. The power of being a man. The control.

Somehow, we missed the memo growing up that it does not have to be that way. Our plumbing is in reality the only biological difference. Our minds, souls, emotions, needs are no less than a man's. It's a journey that is more about changing your way of viewing life and how you fit in it.

To some of you, this is a reaffirmation of things you've already thought. To others, this is a whole alternative world. A massive paradigm shift in the way you think. A way that instinctively may feel wrong or improper. Remember, the way you think is likely based on values that originated from the days of the cave dweller/woman. Unless you still walk around carrying a club, those days are over. And so, the days of the good little girl are over too.

Rejoice in being a woman. We are the future. Now is the time to claim our share of the man kingdom. Now is the time to make things right and fair. I hope that this book will not only open your eyes and motivate you to think differently. My ultimate goal is that you take action. Talking, thinking, reading. They are all necessary. But the actions you take will drive the next generation of women into an age of complete equality, not the pretend facade we still live in.

I should clarify it that not all women can be a bad girl, just like all men can't be a bad boy. Many are happy to just accept the passive role and have fate direct their life. To those of you, my deepest condolences. I only hope that you will at least impart a different set of values to your children so the cycle does not repeat itself.

I should also note that not all men want a bad girl. Just like not all women want a bad boy. Some men want the gentle, sweet flower that complies to his every whim. This makes for a splendid wife that he can walk all over. Whatever floats your boat.

I know it sounds cold. To some extent, it is. But only in the need for equality. Being a bad girl does not imply being mean or loveless. A bad girl gets what she wants, how she wants, on her terms, using her feminine ways to do so. Just like the bad boy in the masculine context.

Every reader should ask themselves one question before they proceed. Are you willing to drop the notion that bad girls are bad people? If you can do that, you're in for a world of growth. If you can not get your head around the idea, the stigmatization, the brainwashing that a bad girl is a bad person, stop reading. Really. I won't be offended. What I just said was that being a bad person? Or just standing my ground and stating the obvious without fear of ruffling some gentle flowers? Welcome to the age of being true to yourself, ladies.

HISTORY LESSON 101

First, there was man. And then man created woman. Wait, what? Exactly. No disrespect to anyone's religious beliefs, but the origins of man and woman are irrelevant to this discussion. What does matter is the origins of man's and woman's psychology? Why do they think the way they do?

Let's break this down into two groups of two - two male groups and two female groups. Alpha (both male and female) and Beta (also male and female). Yes, the traditional breakout of personality types falls under; alpha, beta, omega, gamma, and delta. That's glorious news but has zero relevance to the point being driven here. Omega, Gamma, and Delta personality traits highlight the eccentricity, adventuresomeness, and aloofness a person may display. However, when you dig and dig and dig, ultimately, everyone is alpha or beta at their core.

Alphas are the leaders in life. Beta's, the followers. Yes,

this is a large oversimplification, but it is the core fundamental difference. As for the other groups, they may sort of lead, or sort of follow, but in the end, they are one or the other. That you're quirky or adventurous or like to remain a very private person means nothing in getting what you want out of life.

The default is always beta. Most people are betas at their core. It's easier to walk through life just following the path already carved out for you. For women, they ingrain this beta mindset from the moment they leave the hospital as a newborn. Sadly, as of this publishing, there is no official study conducted to determine the percentages, but making an educated guess, I'd say over 80% of both genders fall primarily in the world of beta. It's important to remember this is a sliding scale. Very few people are at either extreme.

This makes sense when you think about it. Most people are not leaders (in politics or business). Large groups of people follow the few "chosen ones" that lead them to a common goal. However, this leadership does not end in the workplace. When you get home, who does the work to cook and clean? (And who's issuing the 'supervision' of said duties) Who monitors and allows cash flow purchases? Who picks the TV show if you're both in the same room?

The leadership concept carries on to the most menial of daily tasks. This is where most of us see the real underlying threads of our upbringing and our self-expectations. To use the over-used cliche, "who wears the pants in the house", is what we're talking about. So where is this all taking us? The point of looking back is to see the present and the future roles that women voluntarily place themselves in.

We need to start the way we mean to finish. If you start a relationship embracing a self-sacrificing and subservient role, you will probably remain there your entire life. At work, and home. Your outside world is always a manifestation of your inside world, the way you think and feel.

If you want to break free of the chains, the escape starts not with your outward actions but with your inward thoughts about you and how you want to see your life unfold. It is a lot harder said than done, but it is the only real, sustainable course of action to take, that will welcome you to the boys club with both arms open.

One last point I'd like to make. Sit down, perhaps ask for someone to assist you. Take a huge deep breath and then quickly, without hesitation, remove the massive chip off your shoulder. You heard me correctly. You are the master of your domain. The choices you make in this life are your choices, no one else. If you choose to simply accept that women have had a raw deal through history, you would be correct. But also choosing to do nothing about changing it is owned by you. That was then, this is now.

I'm fed up hearing story after story of various groups complaining about how their life is unfair or unjust because of how history has treated them. In almost all cases, the historical tragedies are completely valid. But last time I checked, history has no impact on future events. Our current actions do. Stop complaining and start doing.

If you want more in life. If you want the power, freedom, and control of a man, your role as the 'traditional woman' can not exist in its historically molded form. It simply can not work. The rules of engagement between the genders need to be shaken, not stirred.

A bad girl is a girl that has embraced this knowledge and will let go of the fairytale notion of being a good little girl. Again, this does not mean you need to become a bad person. You just need to relinquish the good girl mores and forget being the wind beneath your man's wings. You have wings of your own. Use them damnit.

SO WHAT'S A 'BAD GIRL' ANYWAY?

I'm thinking liar, cheater, thief? No morals? These would all be as accurate as saying gravity is a conspiracy. According to the Urban Dictionary, a 'good girl' is typically a virgin, never swears, is respectful, and is usually intelligent. Using the same dictionary, a 'good boy' is too good, precious, and pure for this world. Now please stop reading for a second and re-read the above. I did not just make this up. This is real, ladies.

Maybe I just got unlucky? Let's check with Miriam Webster's dictionary on 'bad boy'. "It is a person who flouts convention". And for 'bad girl'? Ooops, would you look at that, there is no definition.

Even using the oh-so modern and technically innovative and forward-thinking resources of the internet, it serves a massively skewed picture in the most subtle and accepting terms. We love to embrace the bad boy and the good boy and good girl. But let's just avoid the bad girl 'cause, ya know, we can't have that now, can we?

If my writing sounds like I'm angry, it's because I am. Why are so few people talking about this? See chapter Two - because 'it's just the way it is'? This is unacceptable at any level. In reality, the word on the street is the bad girl is a more politically correct way to call a woman a slut. But wait, a bad boy is... what was it? Oh ya, "a person who flouts convention". In English, they go against tradition. That's it. That's all. Seriously?

If you're not upset at this point, I'm confident this book will be of no use to you. In essence, you're comfortable knowing it's all good for men to follow a path that goes against tradition, and for women, there is no formal acknowledgment that this behavior even exists and if it does....'well then, she must be a slut'. Yes, your cool with that, then bye-bye.

For all the readers left, seeing as there is no definitive source to define a bad girl, let's build one here.

A bad girl (using the male version as a reference point) is a female that goes against tradition without regard. They march to the beat of their own drum. Whether that be her choice of career path, the style of clothes she wears, the values she embraces in life, the number or frequency of sexual partners she may have, the places she visits. It's all-encompassing. You do you and take whatever steps to achieve it. That's all. You don't do what is expected of you or what you were told you should do when you were a little girl.

Now, using this as a loose operating definition, is anything above wrong or offensive? Does anything above make you a bad person? Sadly, many closed-minded folks would argue the devil has possessed you. Can I get a hallelujah? NOT!

This kind of thinking is as ridiculous as it is offensive.

So why has this truly bassackwards way of thinking been accepted for so long? History, perseverance, and complacency. We, as women, have no control over the past. We have limited control over the systems in place that currently feeds the perseverance. Complacency is the only thing that is 100% within our complete control at all times.

Do you just accept it, or do you do something about it?

For the life of me, I can not understand why every woman would not want to be a 'bad girl'. Unless you have no self-identity, no goals and aspirations superseding others, this should be a no-brainer.

Once you find your inner female power, you will quickly realize it's a lot easier than you thought. So easy and so effective, you may feel guilty. Part of the female psyche is an inner belief that life must be hard. I call it the Cinderella syndrome. To achieve happiness and success, you have to endure copious amounts of hardship and unfairness. Forget Cinderella. Think of every unfair injustice and ask yourself, did it have to be that way?

THE OXYMORON

The icing on the cake? Most men PREFER a 'bad girl'. Say what? Stay with me here.

Even although we are taught and encouraged to be good little girls, most men strongly prefer a woman to be a bad girl at their core. How is this possible and how can we prove this? Take your pick of any media source you want.

Any corner of the web. TV commercials. Any sitcom you can think of. Even the selection of books being produced and published that are likely where you found this book. Our culture runs on two distinctly different levels. To step out and use some academia from my college days, Erving Goffman's book "The Presentation Of Self In Everyday Life", we have a front stage and a backstage to our lives.

The front stage appears on the surface to the public at large. The backstage is what's really going on in our hearts and minds. An example? You've just fought with your parents/friend/spouse. Inside, you feel angry/hurt. You go to the store and bump into someone from work. You appear happy and pleasant like life is good. Inside you may fume with rage or whatever, but your outside behavior (your front stage) is the polar opposite of your actual feelings.

Most men appear to find a bad girl unacceptable and frowned upon. But these are the same men who would likely cheat on you with the same women they condemn. Who do you think captivates their attention more in a mall or at work? Who do you think they admire and respect more? You? Good little girl Suzy? NOT EVEN CLOSE.

Most men get caught in the same nonsensical loop as women. They seek a life partner that is a good little girl. It reinforces them of their decisions by friends and family when they meet Miss prospective spouse. They get married and then... they are bored out of their minds and focus their entire attention on the bad girl at work/school/club.

It's an incredibly sad statistic that 40% of all marriages in America end in divorce. The primary cause is not surprising - infidelity. Either one or both parties cheat. They cheat because they are with the wrong person or because they both act one way on the surface, but think another way deep inside, usually unaware of it themselves.

We all act to be congruent with the way we think and feel. Unfortunately, the bad girl very often is a concept that both men and women try to suppress and not acknowledge.

This is where you should get confused. Like, what is the woman trying to say?

It is in the best interest of most women to want to be a bad girl for both genders' sakes. Yet both men and women have pushed the concept down and cast major negative stigmatization forever and a day.

Women want it. Men love it. Both condemn it. Makes perfect nonsense, but somehow, this is where we are at in our culture.

You picked up this book likely because, at some level, you have intuitively felt the desire to be a bad girl or you have noticed that bad girls seem to always come up on top. They get the best jobs, the best men, the happiest lives. It just doesn't add up.

The balance of this book will look at actionable steps you can take to move out of the good little girl headspace and embrace the inner bad girl. Your pre-programmed instinct will be to fight me (or more accurately, yourself) the entire journey. Please, if nothing else, try to dispose of the preconceived notions you may have had about what is proper and right for women. We are so close to a major paradigm shift in our culture.

The female led relationship, the female led business, and the female focussed culture has always been here. It's just been harnessed by our male counterparts. We need to take back control of our own destiny's and understand there is nothing bad about being a 'bad girl'. Unless, of course, taking back the power and control over men is a bad thing? (Lol)

SO WOMEN ARE SUPERIOR?

Absolutely, NOT! Contrary to what you may think, this is not a book about female superiority. Blacks, Whites, Jewish, Christian, straight, gay. No matter what you label yourself, we all have one thing in common. WE ARE HUMAN. That means, despite our differences, we are all from the same species.

What I am saying is 'bad girls' are most definitely superior to 'good girls'. To be clear, the word 'superior' is defined as higher in social rank, importance, and quality. Good girls are, in my mind, puppets. They do as they're told and we all live happily ever after, right?

Men and women use a different operating system in what motivates them to take any action or decision. This is key. Women work more on emotional processing and men try to work more on logic. A bad girl flips this upside-down whenever it suits her.

Women genetically are usually not as physically strong

as men. Conversely, I've heard it said many times that women's tolerance to pain (childbirth being a perfect example) exceeds that of men. So we have some limitations with each gender. Neither makes it a justification for superiority. Just different strengths.

The bad girl takes the strengths she already has and harnesses them to her advantage. Nothing else. No complicated, high altitude math here. Plain and simple. Where things get sticky is the giving permitting herself to do so.

Sidebar for a moment.

Let's pretend your current job responsibilities did not change. No extra tasks, no longer hours. Now let's pretend they gave you a 20% pay increase... but everyone else you work with did not receive the raise AND they did not know about your pay bump. Would you feel icky? Would you feel guilty showing up for work, knowing you just got an enormous increase "just because"? No? Okay, now let's make that raise 1000% - you now make some ridiculous amount per hour. Let's say you make $1500/hour to stock the shelves alongside Thelma and Billy - both still making their minimum wage. Would you feel guilty? Would you feel you don't deserve the money or that it's unfair that life has thrown you a winning lottery ticket?

Given enough time to think it through, most of you would feel you don't deserve it, and guilt would plague you. Maybe not right away. But give it enough time. You did nothing wrong. You are not doing anything extra. You just happened to be blessed with an HR department that thinks you deserve the money. A reason for which is frankly none of your business or concern. And yet, you feel wrong/bad/guilty.

This is the distinguishing factor between the genders. Men will take what is rightfully theirs. If they're offered the money, then by default it is now theirs to take. The 'good girl' feels not worthy of this windfall. It defies the need to have hardship and disparity-the things all good girls must endure.

The superiority is not between genders. It is between yourself, your definitions, and your expectations. You need to let go of all the baggage they rammed down your throat as a child. Fast-forwarding your life is not wrong. Depriving yourself gives you no awards, banners, or certificates. It's just masochism under a 'good girl' veil.

THE PLAIN AND SIMPLE TRUTH

Y ou picked up this book why? Well, for starters, the title may have grabbed your attention. "Bad Girl - The Guide To Female Power". You may have started reading this book because the blurb promised solutions to gain power and control in your relationships and in life.

The truth is, you likely would have ripped past this book if it was for any of the above alone. No. You likely stopped and started reading because of one primary reason only. The cover. Adam, Eve and the forbidden apple.

That should tell you something right there. You already had an idea where the book was going and wanted to see how the author got you there. Unless you've been living under a rock since who knows when, we all know sex sells. But does it sell to both genders? Actually, no, it doesn't. Stepping back a few chapters, women operate with their hearts and emotions. Men think logically.

Write this down... men think logically BUT, that is ONLY when they are thinking at all. Depending on the study you want to cite, men think about sex between 14 to 20 times a day. For women, this number drops to approximately 6-10 times/day. The urban myth of 'every 7 seconds' was disproven a few decades ago.

What is more revealing is the power of those thoughts. How long do you think Adam contemplated accepting the apple from Eve? (Forgive me using the Christian parable here. Each religion has its own story of comparable sentiments). Adam may have only considered the apple dilemma for a few seconds. It was not the length of time, or how often he considered taking the apple. Once was enough. It was the sheer power of Eve's seduction that pushed him over.

A man's thoughts of sex may not be as often as once first thought, but the power they hold over his actions and decisions are enormous. A woman's sexual energy is the kryptonite to every straight man. Likewise, her sexual energy is also effective for other women and those of non-heterosexual orientation.

Again, don't believe me? Spend 2 hours in a club, watching TV, walking through a shopping center. Female sexuality is the prime number always, everywhere. It is such effective energy, any company that can use it to harness increased sales does so. The tobacco industry was one of the first to truly capitalize on this during the late 50s and early 60s. They converted over half the first world population before they declared it addictive and deadly. They did this almost exclusively by selling the product as a sexually symbolic activity. On the surface, they aimed it at women, but magically, it increased sales for both genders and regardless of sexual orientation. That must have been luck, right? Ya, okay. They spent more than the US National defense budget during the Cold War on advertising: BECAUSE SEX WASN'T WORKING TO CONVERT EVERYONE? Not!

Here's the thing. You likely already know all this. You already know that you can get your guy to go your way. You can get the job if you sex up your wardrobe during the interview. You know you can persuade your friends to see the movie you want over their choices when you exude a highly charged sexual confidence in your request. But you don't.

May I ask, why the hell not? Oh, right. That would make you a manipulative bitch? Do we need to go back over the previous chapters? A woman's sexuality and sexual energy are the undercurrents to all that is human. Own it. Be proud of it. And for the love of whatever God you believe in, USE IT.

Remember the pre-programmed notion that 'good girls' must suffer and be proper and blah blah blah. That is what's holding you back. I used to feel so guilty and ashamed when I first went in this direction. It made me feel dirty and almost worthless. Like it was not cool to use this unfair advantage. Um, you read about the job and the ridiculous raise mentioned earlier?

Our thinking has got to change. There is nothing wrong with exuding sexual energy. Unless you think it's wrong for both genders. The last time I checked, that was a key ingredient that bad boys have. We love it. We embrace it. We adorn it. Hence the immortalization of the famous James Dean figure that has been gone FOR ALMOST 70 YEARS. Wake up, smell the coffee beans and let's get started.

CANDY FROM A BABY

The male specimen is so easy to motivate. Let's face it, they are wonderful, kind, and loyal (usually), but if you know how to push their buttons, you can have your way 100% of the time, no questions asked. Not that you would need or want to do that, but it's there if you need it.

The thing is, few know that most men also prefer the woman in their life to be bad. Again, I'm not talking about being a slut or manipulating his every decision. I'm referring to the bad girl mindset. The confident and almost fearless woman that is not afraid to do what she wants with no reluctance, use her sexual energy to get it if needed.

Need proof? For the single ladies, find a random store that has primarily male associates employed. Gently flirt with one associate with a specific product. Have him leave to 'check for stock'. Immediately on his departure, begin flirting equally with a second or even third associate. When the first returns, watch the in-house awkwardness between the associates, vying for your attention. Make sure the item is a low-cost item, so the commission is not a factor.

For married women, try suggesting a movie you know he will not want to watch. Now embark on some heavier flirting with implications that a payoff will come for him, should he comply with your needs.

Both seem obvious and simple. But what you may fail to recognize is the men involved in this brief experiment will probably enjoy it just as much as you. To be clear, not all men. Just as not all women like a 'bad boy' not all men want the sexual powerhouse that any woman can harness with little effort or imagination. For the men that are not appreciative of a 'bad girl', make sure before you give up.

Some need, how shall I put it... training. They need to gain a taste for it. For all the women not in a committed relationship, acceptance is all you can do. Either accept the guy is a knob or he's a knob. Did I mention he's probably a knob?

For everyone in a committed relationship, try getting your way in a 'bad girl' context 2-3 times. Assuming you have a relationship that you are close enough to have an open discussion, sit down and talk. Tell him what you've been up to. That you think he may like you more as a 'bad girl'. It will shock most of you at the response you receive. For those of you that are with someone who does not appreciate you in that light, sadly, you're stuck. Perhaps a gentler approach may be required over a longer period?

Just remember, you're not a bad person for testing the waters.

Try to imagine being with someone who is 'motivated' by a bad girl approach and PREFERS a bad girl. You get your way and you indirectly please him at the same time. Does it get sweeter?

BALLS

Big hairy balls. That is something that you rarely see as the beginning line of a chapter. Ask me if I care. What does it mean? I think we can all assume the worst.

Having "balls" has been around as an expression in North American culture for several decades. It's even used to describe some women... "She's got balls". But what does it mean? The obvious is guts, courage, bravery, and a willingness to stick one's neck out.

Wait, wait, wait a minute. So we have other words in the English language to use that are the same thing as "balls" - a part of the male genitalia. I guess 'balls' must mean more? IT DOES NOT. But we all use it.

Why?

Why do you think? Courage, bravery, a willingness to stick one's neck out - these are all attributes that are closely aligned to what we accept as male-oriented attributes. WHAT THE FUCK. So women aren't brave? Seriously, how many times do I need to bring attention to the fact that our culture is so deeply up the ass of the male kingdom, even in the most innocent and insidious ways? This expression of having balls may be offensive to some of you, but like it or not, it's used daily by most.

By itself, it's not a big deal. What is the big deal is the compounding of ingrained cultural values that reinforce the need for men to carve their own way and not fear stomping on a few to get there. Meanwhile, it reinforces women to remain quiet little puppets. Few women I know would take being told they have balls as complimentary.

This is the bedrock of our journey.

Grow a set. Now. If you think being a 'bad girl would not be a bit of a bumpy ride, you would be sadly mistaken. It is not the path of least resistance. At least not at first. You need to have inner strength and courage in yourself, your decisions, and your actions.

Every step, every action, every word is going to go against the inner 'good girl' voice inside of you. You will probably have many internal dialogues with yourself, insisting that this is all wrong or silly or just doesn't feel right. Guess what? Your voice would be correct because that voice has been shouting at you since childhood. It's the Malibu Barbie meets Dora The Explorer meets Cinderella voice. X amount of years of societal programming is a lot.

I hope that I have unpacked some of that programming, at least in a theoretical context, up to this point. However, no amount of talking or thinking will overcome the need to conform with the self-identity that has largely been pre-built for you, courtesy of a male-dominated world since the beginning of time.

It is this inner voice that will be your biggest opponent. Your most adamant nemesis. You will not get past yourself unless you have courage, inner strength, a desire to go beyond the expected, and... have a healthy set of balls between your legs.

I say all this as a precursor to what lies ahead. Some of you will feel lost or uncomfortable as we go. If you feel that way, it's okay. I will not hold it against you. I would pause where you're at and revisit this chapter. There is a very good chance you feel uncomfortable because we will be moving horizontally, outside the normal or traditional way of thinking. Your inner 'good girl' voice will be shouting, maybe even screaming at you.

Two things need to take place if that happens. One; why is the voice pushing you away? Because it's wrong, immoral, or just very uncomfortable and scary. Two; if it is because of discomfort or fear, you need to push past it. Courage is not just a good thing to make massive life changes. It's a full-on requirement. Without it, no long-lasting genuine changes will ever occur. This goes with anything in life.

STEP ONE TO STEP OFF

I t should be crystal clear to you. The first and perhaps single most important step to becoming a 'bad girl' is knowing that there is nothing wrong with it and giving yourself mental and emotional permission. Your biggest obstacle is you. Not men, other women, or society. It's you.

Until you tick this box and are ready to move forward, it will always pull you back to the 'good girl'. Even if you can take steps suggested later in this book, eventually you'll come crashing back down to feeling guilty or bad or whatever. You will reset to ground zero. My recommendation is you deal with this first.

Spend some time with yourself and examine why you feel reluctant to depart from being a 'good girl'. Sadly, some of you may never get past this point. If so, that's okay. You can't be someone you're not. The programming of our culture runs long and deep. Accept yourself as you are and move on. But please remember, you have come this far that you have even considered it. Do not resent the women who could crash through these barriers. Praise them. Admire them. Become best friends with them. You never know, they may help you move forward at some point later on.

Once you have resolved the internal conflict, moving forward just gets easier and more effective as you go. I promise you, you will reflect on the days when you felt compelled to play it safe, conforming to the man-driven world, and laugh at yourself. You will wonder how and why you waited so long to utilize the gifts that you were born with.

Step 2 assumes you are now ready to make some outward changes. You have aligned your internal head-space to the outer way you should look and behave. This means you're ready to accept that your okay using your 'get out of jail free' card whenever it suits you, and you will no longer feel guilty or bad for doing so.

As the saying goes, looks are everything, at least for men it is. This is perhaps the easiest and most straightforward way to move outside your head. If you look sexy, you feel sexy. If you feel sexy, you act sexy. You see where we're going with this.

This, in no way, is implying that you need to dress up for the club. Absolutely not. What it means is you need to be mindful of your appearance and how it accentuates your sexual energy. If you walk around in track pants and a sweatshirt all the time, I don't care how naturally beautiful you are; you exude nothing but good girl vibes NO MATTER WHAT. And that's okay... when you don't care or don't need to get what you want.

Spending your Sunday morning curled up on the couch with a delightful book (like this one:) and a cup of coffee demands this attire. Frankly, who cares at that point? But what about when you go to see your boyfriend or to the store or even to the gym? Switching this kind of look to a tank top and LuLu Lemons is a whole alternative world. Both are in athletic attire. But one screams sexuality, the other, not so much.

We could say the same for hair and makeup. If you're studying for exams, doing your taxes, or walking the dog by yourself, no one cares. A messy bun and chapstick work great. If you don't need to use the power, don't. We all need our downtime to just relax and focus on ourselves.

It's important to note that looking good is not the primary thing here. It is the when, the why, and the how. People notice when you have made additional efforts. I'm going to repeat that. They notice. That's plug number one.

People rarely know why you've made yourself presentable or not. It's an unconscious point that is mostly just accepted. Over time, if you are most often seen by others as lazy or bummy in how you keep yourself, they form an unconscious opinion of you that is either favorable or not.

This leads me to my third point, the how. How often you disregard your outward appearance as unimportant will impact your success in shifting people's opinions of you. Specifically, men's opinions, but this goes to both genders to some extent.

Let's pause for a moment. Think of someone you know you would confidently say is a 'bad girl' currently in your life. You may not be besties. You may only know them from a distance. Are they always dressed to kill? Probably not. But we rarely see them without some sense of vanity, and when they dress up, everyone notices. Go big or go home ladies.

Being mindful of the way you look daily should be obvious, but sadly, I've seen many of my girlfriends still not appreciate the power of visual impact. We'll all go out for coffee and I'm the one that gets the free muffin. Not because I ordered it. Because I'm the one wearing the low cut top when I place my order. Trust me, I'm not half as good-looking as some of my friends, but I get all the attention because I know what men want.

Eye candy is seriously underrated by most women. Men love it. Women hate it. Why? I'm convinced it's a combination of low self-confidence and yes, the inner need to stay in the 'good girl' lane no matter what. This is ludicrous.

The point in all of this is looks count. They are not what makes a 'bad girl' but they are the first fundamental piece. If you are not willing to sex up your wardrobe, your journey will be twice as hard. Do not kid yourself. Everyone notices. You may try to convince yourself that it's not that important or that you shouldn't have to do it but stop and think for a second. Pick up any book for men that teaches them how to 'catch a woman' or 'how to become an alpha male' or 'how to get what they want out of life' etc etc, etc. One of the first lessons they're taught is the importance of looking good.

If you think women are void of the same social dynamics, you're in deep denial of the reality of the way we operate. Yes, it is somewhat superficial or shallow. This book was not to address the depth of philosophical existentialism. Get over yourself. If you want to shift your world in a positive, more powerful direction, bad girls are the way to go. Part of that includes caring how you look and accentuating any sexuality you have, whenever possible.

To repeat, this does not mean you need to look like a slut or that you need to dress up 24/7. It simply means appearance counts. The more you understand it, respect it and practice it, the easier things down the road become.

ATTITUDE IS KING

Have you ever found you like someone or dislike them and you do not know why? You may have only spoken to them for a moment, or perhaps you haven't even talked to them at all. You just like them or not.

If you answered no, you are lying to yourself. Seriously, stop reading this book and go home. You are trapped in the good little girls don't cry headspace and we have no time for you. Do you see what I just did? I said what was in my head. I was honest and did not care if it pissed someone off. That's attitude.

Attitude shows itself at every level of a person's being. Their attitude is displayed by how they dress (see previous chapter), by how and what they say, by their actions in a situation. It says something without saying anything in particular.

Good girls pride themselves on vanilla. Vanilla attire,

activities, and most definitely, vanilla attitudes. This is where good girls shine. They are the epitome of attitudelessness (and yes, that is not an actual word). They have no attitude. They love to 'go with the flow' and just be little dainty flowers on the wall of life where they get painted over with each new family that moves in.

Do not confuse attitude with opinion. Everyone has opinions, but not attitudes. Good girl or bad girl, they both have opinions that may or may not agree. Attitude is the mark of the devil to the good girl. That would cause people to step up and notice. It risks ticking a few people off. It may even cause some people to not like her. So she plays in the safe zone of vanilla blankness and lets fate largely be the compass to her life.

Being a 'bad girl' requires a fearless embracement of attitude. The more, the better. The attitude does not have to be disrespectful or contentious. It does not have to be out of alignment with anyone else. All that it has to be is NOTICABLE. The acknowledgment that it exists by those around you. That's it. No rocket science. Nothing bad or controversial. But feared immensely by most.

Why is it feared? Because it has the potential to make you stick out. It's prickly. It's a thing that only Alpha males do. No one else may do that, right? Ya, okay. That's what a good girl wants to believe. It's just not proper to stand out. Please tell me this mentality is no longer. Sadly, I've seen it over and over. With both genders.

We live in a world of over-concern. Politically correct is largely a euphemism for saying you're scared to rock the boat. You don't want to be "THE ONE" that upsets or offends others, even if it's true. This is not a license for being insensitive or reckless in your words. What I am suggesting is you recognize we have become so fearful of standing our ground that we have used being politically correct as the bubble wrap excuse.

A 'bad girl' is a bad girl for many reasons. How she dresses, her words, her actions. It is her attitude that is the defining element. This separates her from her peers more than anything else. She has an attitude. She knows it. Everyone around her knows it. And she is proud of it.

This is the outward expression of the inward manifestations of courage and desire discussed in 'Balls'. Take a moment and again reflect on your 'bad girl' role models in your life. Do they have an attitude? Damn straight they do. It is the "je ne sais quoi" (French translated to mean 'something that can't be described with words') that radiates from every inch of their persona.

A bad girl attitude is magnetic and yet frowned upon. The "I don't give a shit what you think, this is what I want, and I will get it, no matter what, and we both know that so stop fighting me and move over" tone in almost everything they say and do. I remember the first time I consciously tried to come off this way. It was in, of all places, a car dealership. I think I saved close to $2000 with this approach. Mind you, I'm sure the short miniskirt and heels didn't hurt either :)

The attitude should come from a place of expectation, not wants, needs or redirection. In all things said and done, bad girls expect everything to go their way. They don't try to make it happen. They don't try to force it to happen. They EXPECT it. You are invincible. You are not bad or manipulative or demanding. You simply see no other options beyond your expectations of how things will play out. This is the attitude you need.

It seems simple, but it requires a high degree of work and effort. As with all things in life, the more you do it, the easier and more natural it becomes. The easiest way to move forward is through small baby steps. Each day is a fresh way.

REBEL IS AS REBEL DOES

At this point, you dare to move forward, you have fearlessly developed the look and the attitude. Now what? Now you put things into action. This is where the 'bad girl' is defined by an outsider looking in. Where you get what you want.

The power of being female is not that we have the proverbial apple. The power is what we do with it. Do we take a bite and say "here, have some"? Or do we offer it up with the underlying, unspoken hint of sexuality through seduction?

Nothing is more intriguing than the hint of a promise. Notice, I did not say the act of something, I specifically said "hint". You could wrap this up in a bow and call it a flirtation, but this is too crude and flagrant. It must be subtle. It must be below the surface of an actual flirtation. Everyone's reality is a function of their perception. If people perceive something, then it becomes their reality. You want to lie below outright flirting, at least, initially.

Let's take another step backward for a second. The single most effective way historically to motivate men (primarily) and women is by playing to their sexual needs. Remember the advertising they bombard you with daily. Literally, trillions of dollars have been spent over the last five decades. I'm going to repeat that. TRILLIONS, with a T. This amount of money, is not spent because it does not work.

You may not like the idea. You may strongly object to it. Perhaps you see it as unethical? Like gravity, agree or disagree with it, it is a reality to life. The beautiful aspect to all this? Most men are impervious to its power. They just can't say no. It's part of their biological makeup.

So why are we not harnessing this to our advantage? Oh, right. Because that would be wrong, out of bounds, not following the 'good girl' handbook. The fact that we have been blessed with being born female is not our fault nor within our control. You did not ask to be born female. It just is. It makes little sense to handicap yourself BECAUSE you were born that way.

You were born with the gift of being able to tap into female sexuality. Men have been born with an innate and insatiable need to seek this sexuality. You hint at it, through your attitude, your words, your style, your actions, and they become putty in your hands.

No one can tell me this is something new you didn't already know. We all know it. Very few come out and say it in such crude, mechanical terms, but there it is. If you feel guilty for having this innate power, I suspect you would feel equally guilty being born into a wealthy family or winning the lottery. You did nothing to deserve it, it just happened out of random luck.

Here's where things get sticky. Knowing it's there, and assuming you don't feel guilty about it, why are we not using it? As with all obstacles in life, the single biggest reason anyone does not move forward... fear. Fear of what others will think. Fear of being rejected by your moves being disregarded. Fear of going against the 'good girl' mentality they have raised you to believe is the way it has to be.

I get it. It is scary to think your female sexual power is not powerful at all. The 'what if I flirt and the guy/boyfriend/hubby takes no notice' voice in your head. Remember, I did not say flirt. At no point are you flirting with anyone. How can you feel rejected if you're not outwardly flirting?

To be clear, I'm suggesting we use our sexual energy in the subtlest and indirect ways that are sexual BUT not flirting. Examples? Drop something on the floor, bend over making sure the top of your thong is visible as you go to pick it up. Speaking in a soft, gentle, almost melodic tone. How you smell. Opening your purse to get something, make sure you have a condom or piece of lingerie visible as you dive in to look. Tapping your newly manicured nails on the counter as you wait for them to look up the inventory supply. Pouting your lips, perhaps even slowly licking them as you contemplate the action they've just asked you to take.

The above list is not comprehensive, but I hope makes the point. None of those actions have you directly flirting. In several of the examples, you're not even directly engaged with the other person. You are just introducing tiny sensory cues that exude sexuality. I do most in an "oops" kind of innocent way.

Your 'innocent sexuality' may go unnoticed or prove ineffective, but why would you not test the waters and try. It would amaze you how much a man's disposition to me changes, the second I oh so accidentally make sure he sees my G-string. I have caught myself laughing after the fact because it has become such a simple way to plug into their weak spot. My wish becomes their every command in a matter of seconds.

It's important to understand that the mere act of this kind of behavior is unlikely to work by itself. It's a package deal. Attitude, the way you dress/look at that moment, and frankly, practice. Do not give up if it fails on a first attempt. Look at being a 'bad girl' as not individual acts, but as a way of living. Over time, things just fit together seamlessly. Things that you have to proactively think about doing today, become a natural part of your being over time.

Depending on how badly you want your way and the relationship you have with the person you want to persuade, the degree of indirect sexuality can shift. You don't have to rely on the subtle all the time. Sometimes, you just need to shift into top gear to get what you want.

BAD BOY MEETS BAD GIRL

What happens if you have worked hard to break free of the 'good girl' headspace and you meet a bad boy? Even better, what happens if you're with a bad boy and you decide to stop following the 'good girl' path? Is this a spark or explosions mix?

The truth is, it is likely extremely colorful. Beyond that, each couple is as individual as your fingerprint. For some, it will prove magical. You both feed off the energy of each other. You both share the alpha gene and both want to lead and control. This is not necessarily a bad thing. A lot of bad boys want a woman who knows what she wants and knows exactly how to get it. It becomes an aphrodisiac to them. They are bad boys BECAUSE they want to attract the bad girl.

Conversely, some bad boys want a good little girl / submissive puppet. They want their cake and they want to eat it too. Sadly, this would be the majority. This kind of dynamic can prove to be more of a power struggle versus a power enhancement. A fight for control looms around every corner of the relationship.

If you have found yourself with a man that is of the latter dynamic, you need to accept the choices you made much earlier in the relationship. You wanted a bad boy. You liked his way of taking charge and breaking the rules to get his way. You felt drawn to his seductive way of manipulating you. Now, you want to turn that around. But he wants the soft and submissive good girl you once were. You may need to make some hard choices about the future of the relationship. You either accept your subservient status for the duration you are together. Or you end the relationship before things get potentially hostile.

Notice how you wanted to be with the bad boy, even when you were a good girl. But, but, but... the same is the case with 95% of the guys you want and should be with. They WANT a 'bad girl'. To them, the 'bad girl' is just out of their reach. They are not good enough (in their minds).

The combinations and permutations of what types of people will or will not work are endless. If you are in a relationship or are looking for a relationship, the man that will be most receptive to the 'bad girl' is more of black magic than a hardcore science. The same as with women and the bad boy. Many love it. They love the rebellious, slightly broken, aggressive, and manipulative man. They instinctively know he's no good, but they just can't help themselves in resisting. (This works the same way for us as 'bad girls' btw). There are also some women that just don't have the time for the head games and drama a bad boy is likely to bring to the table. The deciding factor is the individual, nothing else.

What all this should tell you is that you have no control over other people's tastes, weaknesses, and desires. The only thing you have complete control over is yourself and your actions/thoughts. Becoming a 'bad girl' is a way to help balance the scales. Rarely have I seen any of my friends regret following in my footsteps. As long as they remain true to their set of values and beliefs and acknowledge the deep-rooted values of the past as being archaic and nonsensical in today's world, they always come out on top.

Always be the 'bad girl' only up to the point you feel comfortable. Never go past that or you will probably suffer from a massive identity crisis. Just know, the good little girl is a waste of time and we need to stop ramming this ideology down each generation's throat.

PART-TIME BAD GIRL

Coming to terms with the reality of how females are raised can be daunting. Not that anyone is proactively trying to push women down (at least not most). It's just a matter of tradition, repetition and the human condition defaulting to avoid change at all costs.

But what if you like being a good girl? It feels natural. Like it's outside of your skin to explore concepts discussed in here about being a 'bad girl'. A quick revisit to the beginning of this book should remind you that a 'bad girl' is a woman that proactively goes against tradition without regard. She carves her own path.

Typically, that path includes avenues that will prove to help improve the quality of her life, her satisfaction, and her control of outcomes. This does not mean you have to do something. Just knowing what the first several chapters say, and then proactively choosing to remain happy as a good girl has made you a bad girl.

Huh? I presented you with clear, undeniable truths that compel many women to stand up and take notice. Anything less would be sinful. Yet you want to stay as you were. So...is that not going against the groove of expectations? I realize this is a bit of a stretch, but I don't want any readers to feel less of themselves because of their choices. We all need to unite, support each other and lose the judgment gavel of others who go in a different direction.

If you want to dip your toes in the water of 'bad girl' life and show a little more leg than necessary, great! They do not lock you into the jail of badass. You are dipping your toes. The more you use your female sexual energy in a more directed way, the more confidence you gain and the more effective you become. Often, this becomes a snowball effect. More begets, more.

But no one is holding a gun at your head that you must continue or that you must be more aggressive in the art of subtle seduction. No one is forcing you to dress up all the time or to have the "I expect it, therefore, I shall have it" attitude.

Always, always, always be true to your inner self. Anything less than that is an attempt to appeal to men, other women, or the contents of this book. You do you and at the level and extent you want whenever you want.

That all being said, embracing a 'bad girl' persona is rather all-encompassing. The more you allow yourself permission to go there, to be 'bad', the easier it becomes and the more effective it gets. Moreover, with each mini success you have, the more you want. I don't want to suggest that there is an addictive component to it, but it is a rather seductive lifestyle that is hard to turn away from the further along the path you go.

With that, I slowly moved toward 'bad girl' each day. It was not a linear path. There were many days where I suffered from low self-confidence, laziness, or just didn't care enough what the outcome was, for me to put any effort in. As time has passed, that is no longer the case. I now find myself feeling nauseous at the thought of the 'good girl' mentality I once embraced for dear life. I get angry with how we have been indirectly brainwashed to miss so much.

Is being a 'bad girl' a full-time thing? It does not have to be, but it usually happens with time, confidence, success, power, and most importantly, enhanced freedom to do whatever the hell you want in life.

LET'S TALLK ABOUT SEX, BABY

The end game of being a 'bad girl' is what a 'good girl' strives for and never seems to get. Respect, love, happiness, and their way. The more off-center you push your 'bad girl' self and fully embrace the 'bad girl' mentality, the better things become. I know it seems counter-intuitive, but it is true.

Gone are the days of traditional monogamy and all its constraints. The internet blew the lid off all the secret worlds of deviant behavior. If you want to push the envelope beyond the subtle art of seduction, by all means. The fast track to getting your way has always been by appealing to what's between a man's legs.

Please do not misunderstand or misconstrue my words here. I am in no way suggesting you compromise the integrity of your values and beliefs. If you are in a committed relationship and see outward sexual activity at any level as being a form of infidelity, this is where you draw the line. Likewise, I'm not suggesting you have sex with some random person to get your way. To me, that's just short of being a prostitute. Not cool at any level.

What I am saying is, IF you are in an open relationship OR you are single AND you feel comfortable going beyond the previous step because you want some fun for yourself, leverage your desires. If you are in a committed relationship, also consider a degree of leverage that works for you and is comfortable for both of you. This is the defining action that slots many women into a 'bad girl' status by their counterpart 'good girls'.

Let's look at this a little deeper. Why is this a bad thing? Is enjoying sex evil? Not in the least. Are you being asked to cheat? Again, not at all. Cheating is not something this author condones under any circumstances.

Yet, I'm confident I have some readers' faces scrunched up saying "no way!" This goes back to the paradigm of being a 'good girl'. They have trained you to think enjoying sex is wrong if it's just for the sake of enjoyment. I see. So I guess the same standards apply to men? What's that? Does it hold them to a unique set of rules and regulations? Yes, that seems fair and logical.

Drop the programming. Seriously. Open your mind to the possibilities. Imagine the power you will have over men when you take the actual act of sex and throw it into the mix. Not just your sexual energy. Not just your powers of seduction, but the actual act. This is when things jump on the superhighway of power, control, and freedom.

To repeat myself, what I'm suggesting here is using sex when you want to have sex AND it is in line with your moral codes of conduct. If you're going to do it, why not also use it as leverage to get whatever you want in the meantime?

This is a bold departure for the 'good girl' mindset and I have left it until later in the book. It is not the only way, but it is by far the most effective way for both short-term and long-term gains. It is also the symbolic moment of stepping off the 'good girl' ledge.

They have elevated men in social status, even revered them for being promiscuous. Why the hell can't the same be the case for women? Think about it. There is a truth specifically about this mentality that I have alluded to several times throughout this book. In blatant terms, most men prefer a 'bad girl', they just don't know it. Think of any situation where a man's actions are challenged. If he remotely thinks he has a shot with you, he will appease his animal needs over logic, rationalization, or most times, righteousness. Like it or not, it is the truth the over-whelming majority of the time.

BAD GIRL AND THE FEMALE LED RELATIONSHIP

A h, yes. The pinnacle of being a 'bad girl'. This is ultimately where all true 'bad girls' end up. It is the endgame, usually without premeditation or proactive thought. This is the place most women want to end up, but just don't realize it until they are well on their way. The female led relationship.

This is where the 'bad girl' rubber hits the road (I've always wanted to use that expression, but could never find an appropriate place to use it :)). It's where the female is unquestionably in control. This does not mean she is in control in a sexually dominating way (though that is often the case). It means she is the leader. The leader in all the decisions made in the relationship. What to have for dinner, which movie to see, which items should be purchased or passed by. She becomes the literal center of her partners' universe.

Some women don't want that degree of control and

power. It's kind of scary if I'm to be honest. At least, at first. But as you become accustomed to this way of life, it becomes second nature.

Before you leave this book, take a few moments to surf the net, look around the number of blog entries, videos, and books on the topic. FLR (Female Led Relationships). It has blown up. Not because it's the latest and greatest flavor of the day, but because it is the future.

Can you have a good girl in an FLR? I would argue no. They have been self-deprecating, subservient, and self-sacrificing for far too long. FLR demands you put yourself first. Not to suggest you don't love your man and your family, you just love yourself most. A 'bad girl' has learned to embrace selfishness. They have learned that it's not only okay to do so, but that it's considered desirable by most men.

Think about what you like in a man. Do you like a man that is super compliant and bends to your every need at all times? Do you like a puppet? Most women prefer a man that is strong-willed, confident, driven, and fearless. What if you could have that and still be in charge?

Love, care, and concern are not compromised. You can still love, be kind, and caring. You just make sure your needs are always of supreme importance. Again, think about your preferences for a man. For whatever reason, women have lost themselves. FLR is a way to make that reconnection.

I'd like to caution you, however. There are a plethora of books, blogs, and workshops that suggest FLR is a thing you can just jump into. You Can Not. Going from a traditional relationship dynamic it loads an FLR with inherit problems. You need to change the way your mind and heart view the world and open your expectation of possibilities long before you embark on shifting to an FLR.

Remember when you got your first job? It may have been a relatively straightforward job doing menial tasks as a student in high school. Nothing big or fancy, yet you probably had a week or two, before you felt like 'going to work' was normal and natural. Perhaps you remember starting a workout routine. Remember the first month? Did 'working out' feel normal to you or did it feel like it was not a part of who you were, but you just did it, anyway?

My point is, FLR relationships are a monumental shift. You can't just jump in. Your mind needs time to catch up. The 'bad girl' is 95% of the way there and they don't even know it. This transition then becomes a natural evolution and feels like it is the next logical step to how your life should proceed.

I'm currently writing a complimentary book to this one that will examine FLR's in much greater detail. I have included it towards the end of this book to bring your attention to the possibilities a 'bad girl' has available to them if you just say "yes".

ROME WASN'T BUILT

We have established that society has been set up to skew fairness between genders. That there are systemic traditions and life values in place that perpetuate the good girl mentality, despite its archaic and irrational foundations. We have looked at the incremental changes that a woman can make (depending on her comfort) that shift her actions, attitudes, and outcomes. We have looked at fearlessly using the natural sexual energy that lies within every woman, to help persuade any male on the planet. And we have addressed both sexual and social freedom to being a 'bad girl' in the all-encompassing definition, highlighting the subvert preference that most men prefer this kind of woman regardless of what logic would dictate.

The single most important thing to remember is you need to be true to yourself. If the perks of becoming a 'bad girl' strongly appeal to you, but you just can't escape the chains of the good girl mindset, that's okay. It's not your fault. Nor is there anything wrong with it as long as your happy being that way. We should all never compromise who we are inside just because it makes sense to change. Most of us do many things that make no sense at all, yet we continue to do them because it feels right for us.

The intent of my writing this book was to open people's eyes. To make you aware that wanting to be a 'bad girl' is not a bad thing. It's not a wrong thing to want or to do. In most cases, it is empowering and makes your life a whole bunch 'funner' (another word I just made up because I can).

You realize that breaking out of who you are is difficult at first. Your mind will try to trick you at every corner to go back to safety. This is normal. If the feeling becomes overwhelming, then take a few steps back and reevaluate. No two people are the same.

Likewise, it's equally important that you appreciate any changes to who you are, and how you interact with the world will take time. Lots of time. Only go forward at a pace that you are comfortable with and only take baby steps at each stage. As long as you remain true to your own heart and mind, it's all good.

Becoming a bad girl is not a destination. It is a journey that can take a lifetime. It is not a single act or a series of actions where you get some kind of certification or designation from the bad girl society of whateverland. It is a way of life that goes against centuries of flawed thinking.

A bad girl is a bad girl, not by what she does or does not do. She is a bad girl by the way she thinks, feels, and acts on a day-to-day basis. Saying that is huge. It is a complete paradigm shift in how much you value your own life. I think it is prime time that we stop the insanity and stigma attached to this label. Don't feel guilty for wanting to take the apple and offer it up. If you want to, why the hell not? If you don't want to, that's equally cool too.

I hope that if nothing else, this book has opened your eyes. You may not agree with my personal life choices, but I would be deeply disturbed knowing that you think it's good to perpetuate the massive injustice and unfairness that has been given to women since the beginning of time.

If you have found this book helpful, I would be honored and appreciative if you could take a few minutes to write a quick review and/or give it a rating in whichever retail outlet you purchased it from. The more people that do that, the easier it will be for others to find it and benefit. We need to stick together and stop the backstage of male domination once and for all. This would be an awesome first step for you to help.

Thank you so much for your precious time in reading through my rants and tolerating my soapbox moments. Just please remember, a bad girl is not a bad person and a good girl can be a terrible person. That's all that matters to move forward.

I wish you the best of luck.

Hugs,

Allora

ALSO BY ALLORA SINCLAIR

ABOUT THE AUTHOR

Allora Sinclair is a happily married 40 year old mom. She and her loving cuckold husband Dave (davie) have been in a Female Led marriage for over seven years and she has now decided to start documenting their journey. If Allora is not found at her computer or out shopping for a new pair of shoes, she is usually found in the caring arms of davie. She has done a series of non-fiction books to help couples navigate their way through the heavily distorted life of being a cuckold couple. Allora has also done a series of fiction books that are loosely based on some of their real-life adventures. She is now working on a series of books that address and clarify FLR's. This book is the first in the series.